The Twelve
of Christmas

Volume Six

ex libris

Candlestick Press

Published by:
Candlestick Press,
Diversity House, 72 Nottingham Road, Arnold, Nottingham NG5 6LF
www.candlestickpress.co.uk

Design, typesetting, print and production by Diversity Creative
Marketing Solutions Ltd., www.diversitymarketing.co.uk

Introduction and selection © Carol Ann Duffy, 2014

Cover illustration 'Six Geese A-Laying'
© Lizzie Adcock, www.arumliliedesigns.co.uk

© Candlestick Press, 2014

ISBN 978 1 907598 27 2

Acknowledgements:
'Advent' by Carol Ann Duffy is printed here by kind permission of
the author. Our thanks also to James Caruth and smith|doorstop for
permission to reprint 'New Year in Arras' from *The Death of Narrative*
(smith|doorstop, 2014). Andrew Forster, 'Christmas Eve 1969' is
published here for the first time by kind permission of the author. Thanks
to Nancy Campbell for permission to print 'The Hunter's Wife Becomes
The Sun', also for the first time. 'a pint for the true shepherds' by Helen
Mort first appeared in *a pint for the ghost* (tall-lighthouse, 2010) and is
reprinted by kind permission of the author and publisher; our thanks to
Eyewear Publishing for permission to reprint 'The barn swallow's carol'
from *Cape Town*, 2012. Kit Wright, 'Metal, is from *Ode to Didcot Power
Station* (Bloodaxe Books, 2014) and is reprinted by kind permission of the
publisher. Our thanks for permission to reprint 'The Deadly Sins and the
Holy Virtues - No.5 Patience' © Lorraine Mariner from *There Will Be No
More Nonsense* (Picador, 2014). 'On the Birth of Good & Evil During the
Long Winter of '28', copyright © 1976 by Philip Levine; from *They Feed
They Lion* and *The Names Of The Lost: Poems* by Philip Levine. Used
by permission of Alfred A. Knopf, an imprint of the Knopf Doubleday
Publishing Group, a division of Random House LLC. All rights reserved.
Dannie Abse, 'A New Diary', is from *New Selected Poems: Anniversary
Collection (1949-2009)*, Hutchinson, 2009, and is reprinted by permission
of The Random House Group Ltd.

Candlestick Press wishes to thank Carol Ann Duffy for her generosity.

Where poets are no longer living, their dates are given.

A donation from sales of this pamphlet will go to the housing charity
Shelter, www.shelter.org.uk.

Contents
Page

Introduction	*Carol Ann Duffy*	5
New Year in Arras	*James Caruth*	7
On the Birth of Good and Evil during the Long Winter of '28	*Philip Levine*	8
A New Diary	*Dannie Abse*	9
In the Bleak Mid-Winter	*Christina Rossetti*	10
The barn swallow's carol	*Kate Noakes*	11
Metal	*Kit Wright*	12
The Deadly Sins and the Holy Virtues – No. 5 Patience	*Lorraine Mariner*	13
Christmas Eve 1969	*Andrew Forster*	14
a pint for the true shepherds	*Helen Mort*	15
The Burning Babe	*Robert Southwell*	16
The Hunter's Wife Becomes The Sun	*Nancy Campbell*	17
Advent	*Carol Ann Duffy*	19

Introduction

It is a hundred years since the unofficial (and officially unreported) Christmas Truce of 1914, when German and British soldiers along the Western Front downed their weapons and instead greeted each other across no-man's land. Each in their own language sang carols both sides knew and loved or, in one instance, introduced the beautiful 'Stille Nacht' to the world. The words needed no translation. For that Christmas, what was shared between them – their traditions, their humanity, even their beer and schnapps - was greater than what divided them.

It seems fitting, therefore, that this year's selection of Christmas poems should open with James Caruth's 'New Year in Arras', while other poems also explore ideas around war and suffering, the past and the present. And while there is no wallowing in nostalgia, many of the poems this year are about childhood Christmases, family life in all its mishaps and glories, and the magic and beauty that can erupt out of the mundane. In addition to my own poem, there is new work by Nancy Campbell and Andrew Forster. Meanwhile, Robert Southwell's sixteenth-century poem, 'The Burning Babe', a great favourite of mine, introduces the tradition of visionary poetry that flourished in late medieval work and still electrifies.

Many of this year's poems, though they start from different places and speak in different voices, are united by the impulse to extend the hand of friendship, even when this isn't easy, to contrast the warmth of love with the cold of winter. I hope you find the poems full of surprises, delights and food for thought and discussion around the table.

Happy Christmas!

Carol Ann Duffy

New Year in Arras

The Flemish gables show no signs of war,
their detailed reconstruction carried out with care.

The red-brick and grey stone facades,
curlicues and stucco work, the mansards,

appear untouched, and there's no trace of lasting scars
down amongst the restaurants and bars,

all memory of bombardment covered over.
Now, a young man squats in a doorway under cover

of a thin blanket. I drop every coin
I have into his lap, lower my head and walk on.

And I think of my son, New Year at home,
how hard it seems to speak of love on a phone.

James Caruth

On the Birth of Good and Evil during the Long Winter of '28

When the streetcar stalled on Joy Road,
the conductor finished his coffee, puffed
into his overcoat, and went to phone in.
The Hungarian punch press operator wakened
alone, 7000 miles from home, pulled down
his orange cap and set out. If he saw
the winter birds scuffling in the cinders,
if he felt this was the dawn of a new day,
he didn't let on. Where the sidewalks
were unshovelled, he stamped on, raising
his galoshes a little higher with each step.
I came as close as I dared and could hear
only the little gasps as the cold entered
the stained refectory of the breath.
I could see by the way the blue tears squeezed
from the dark of the eyes, by the way
his moustache first dampened and then froze,
that as he turned down Dexter Boulevard,
he considered the hosts of the dead,
and nearest among them, his mother-in-law,
who darkened his table for twenty-seven years
and bruised his wakings. He considered how
before she went off in the winter of '27
she had knitted this cap, knitted so slowly
that Christmas came and went, and now he could
forgive her at last for the twin wool lappets
that closed perfectly on a tiny metal snap
beneath the chin and for making all of it orange.

Philip Levine

A New Diary

This clerk-work, this first January chore
of who's in, who's out. A list to think about
when absences seem to shout, Scandal! Outrage!
So turning to the blank, prefatory page
I transfer most of the names and phone tags
from last year's diary. True, Meadway, Speedwell,
Mountview, are computer-changed into numbers,
and already their pretty names begin to fade
like Morwenna, Julie, Don't-Forget-Me-Kate,
grassy summer girls I once swore love to.
These, whispering others and time will date.
Cancelled, too, a couple someone else betrayed,
one man dying, another mind in rags.
And remembering them my clerk-work flags,
bitterly flags, for all lose, no-one wins,
those in, those out, *this* at the heart of things.
So I stop, ask: whom should I commemorate,
and who, perhaps, is crossing out my name now
from some future diary? Oh my God,
Morwenna, Julie, don't forget me, Kate.

Dannie Abse

In the Bleak Mid-Winter

In the bleak mid-winter, frosty wind made moan;
   Earth stood hard as iron, water like a stone;
Snow had fallen, snow on snow, snow on snow,
   In the bleak mid-winter, long ago.

Our God, Heaven cannot hold Him, nor earth sustain;
   Heaven and earth shall flee away when He comes to reign.
In the bleak mid-winter a stable-place sufficed
   The Lord God Almighty, Jesus Christ.

Enough for Him, whom cherubim worship night and day,
   A breastful of milk, and a mangerful of hay;
Enough for Him, whom angels fall down before,
   The ox and ass and camel which adore.

Angels and archangels may have gathered there,
   Cherubim and seraphim thronged in the air:
But only His mother in her maiden bliss
   Worshipped the Beloved with a kiss.

What can I give Him, poor as I am?
   If I were a shepherd I would bring a lamb;
If I were a wise man I would do my part
   Yet what I can I give Him - give my heart.

Christina Rossetti (1830 – 1894)

The barn swallow's carol

Families gather, but as you come to sing
by the child's crib, I'm far off on the wing,
so long gone south-due-south into the Berg
wind, not hidden, torpid, not cold-air hung.

I don't know of hoar frost, or snow on snow
on snow. Earth-iron, water-stone
are mysteries. Bleak ice makes no moan.

I'm swallow, what gifts can I bring? Fat gnats,
thick mud, new nests from fynbos or Cape Flats.
Mid-winter/mid-summer, all I can I share:
the dip-dive, the soar-swoop in fresh-fly-air.

Kate Noakes

Metal

A steelmill town, a ridge of pine,
  The taste of snow upon the tongue,
Meant all the world was black and white
  At Christmastime when he was young.

In softened angle, muted line,
  The harshnesses became oblique,
The keening lathes were pacified:
  All quiet on the frozen creek.

And it was Christmas when he died
  Far off, no place on earth to go,
But fresh as in his childhood came
  The scent of metal and of snow.

Kit Wright

The Deadly Sins and the Holy Virtues – No. 5 Patience

Our mother had too much faith in us that December, thought my
brother and I could share the Father Christmas advent calendar
with plastic figures waiting behind the doors on his stomach,
with his legs that leapt with joy when we pulled a string. We'd
longed for him – state of the art, owned last year by the coolest
kids – bought to appease us for the birth of our sister.

Two weeks in and we couldn't remember whose turn it
was to open today's door, started bickering. Our sleep deprived
mother went ballistic; tore Santa in two so we could have half
each, miniature pixies scattering across the kitchen. I was still
sobbing when our lift to school knocked at the door.

Coming home that afternoon I'd forgotten the events of the
morning until I encountered Santa in his place on the fridge,
Scotch Tape around his belly, keepsakes back behind the bent
doors, my sister asleep in the warmth of our mother's cooking.
So we started over, with our reassembled, paralysed Santa – my
mum, brother and I with our patched-up earthly forgiveness -
counting the days until Christmas.

Lorraine Mariner

Christmas Eve 1969

Dad and I came here on two buses
to bring Grandma home for Christmas.
Since we set off it's snowed and snowed. Lost
in parka, scarf and gloves, I'm clinging
to his hand in this strange world of concrete
towers where children are all bigger
than me, stares cold as snow on my face.

Grandma's house is dark and Dad's knock is hollow.
We trudge over the white lawn, peek through windows.
The neighbour shouts that Grandma, impatient,
left by taxi when the snow started.
We march back to the bus stop, the streets
vanishing around us in a swirl of white.

Memory will transform this day into
a magical Christmas, but I don't know this
yet. The bus isn't coming. There's a choice:
an endless, bitter walk or be taken
hostage by boys behind lamp-posts, waiting
for Dad to drop his guard. I close my eyes
and see Mum mashing tea in our kitchen,
smell hot mince pies, while my face freezes.

Andrew Forster

a pint for the true shepherds

Now the chance has gone, I wish
I'd bought that man a pint:
the farmer who sat silent next to me
through Midnight Mass, and raised
his eyebrows as the well-fed vicar
revelled in the story of the gentle shepherds
(*friends, how like The Lord's own servants*
are the men round here who still
keep animals today). And as the organist
received the nod to play, the man
who hadn't spoken took his cue at last,
rose to his feet, said: *Reverend,*
tha knows nowt about sheep.

Helen Mort

The Burning Babe

As I in hoary winter's night stood shivering in the snow,
Surprised I was with sudden heat which made my heart to glow;
And lifting up a fearful eye to view what fire was near,
A pretty babe all burning bright did in the air appear;
Who, scorchéd with excessive heat, such floods of tears did shed
As though his floods should quench his flames which with his
tears were fed.
"Alas," quoth he, "but newly born in fiery heats I fry,
Yet none approach to warm their hearts or feel my fire but I!
My faultless breast the furnace is, the fuel wounding thorns,
Love is the fire, and sighs the smoke, the ashes shame and scorns;
The fuel justice layeth on, and mercy blows the coals,
The metal in this furnace wrought are men's defiléd souls,
For which, as now on fire I am to work them to their good,
So will I melt into a bath to wash them in my blood."
With this he vanished out of sight and swiftly shrunk away,
And straight I calléd unto mind that it was Christmas day.

Robert Southwell (ca. 1561 – 1595)

The Hunter's Wife Becomes The Sun

'Don't go without this.' Isabel handed me a small white box
which held a candlestick and four attendant angels.
Jingling clichés punched from sheets of tin,
the angels turn, propelled by heat rising from a candle,
and hooked by their haloes from wires as if the darkness
was a deep pool for fly-fishing, and my window

delicate as ice upon its surface. Spinning by the window,
this carousel recalls a childhood blessing: *Four angels*
at my head. If they came to life, like the small white angels
who fought the Snow Queen's snowflakes, would their tin
armour frighten bears back to the polar darkness?
For whom are the gifts they grasp: tree, star, trumpet, candle?

Only the undertaker sells the right kind of candle
to suit these angels. At home, he wreathes a small white coffin
with plastic lilies, but says nothing. His window
overlooks crucifixes buried in snow; there are no angels
on the graves of the Danes, who came to barter tin
for ivory and sealskin. Their eyes brimmed with darkness,

you see it in old photographs. Sleepless in the darkness,
I read their letters home, those 'tragic accidents'. Green candles
burn beyond the hills: the dead are dancing. The window
between the worlds grows thin. A solar wind blows its low tin whistle
and fire draws closer. Soon earth will be a small white dwarf,
a revolving toy abandoned by its guardian angels.

The candle gutters. Lynched in their own light, the angels
hang still. Each holds her gift before her as if the tin
scorched her fingertips. Heat has melted the small white stump
to nothing. Once, they say, this land was lit by candles
made of ice, when water burned, glazing the darkness
of endless night. Day had not dawned on any window.

The hunter spoke. His cold breath quenched a candle:
'In darkness we are without death.' His wife listened
and replied, 'But we need more light, not darkness,
while we are alive.' She seized a shard of blazing ice
and rose into the sky, scattering a vast white wake
of stars, which some might say were angels,

if, in temperate darkness, we still believed in angels.
The small seal and the white whale know we're just tin gods.
At the world's last window, I light another candle.

Nancy Campbell

Advent

(for Camilla and Beatrice)

One last, silvered leaf fails to fall
from its tree. A hard year's winter
has frozen your voice.

                    You would still rejoice
if you could sing, in your listening church –
where candles thrill to their endings,
light's brave lovers – gold carols
this dark Advent;
                    the hurt heart harkening:

Lo! He comes with clouds descending.

But there is the descant moon
over our scarred world, its cold, pure breve,
and you will sing to your child
                    on Christmas Eve.

Carol Ann Duffy